MW00779825

Escaping the Corner

By Karol M. Wasylyshyn

Behind the Executive Door

Standing on Marbles

Tanto Tempo

Escaping the Corner

...With Other Tales about Leaders Leading and Loving

Karol M. Wasylyshyn, PsyD

Illustrated by
Richard McKnight

For

Stella and Nick

who survived their darkened corners…
and, built a brighter one together

Published by TrueNorth Press, Philadelphia, PA

Wasylyshyn, Karol, M., McKnight, Richard. Escaping the Corner: ...With
Other Tales of Leaders Living and Loving
Philadelphia: TrueNorth Press, 2013.
p. : ill. ; cm.
Summary: Poetic vignettes and allegories focused on business leaders'
habits and relationships.
ISBN: 978-0-9824683-6-4
Library of Congress Control Number: 2012954463
First Edition

Photo of Dr. Wasylyshyn (jacket), by Eli Allen

This book is available at discount when purchased in quantity (15 or
more copies). To inquire, go to
TrueNorthPress.com.

Book design, cover design, and typesetting by Richard McKnight.
Set in Didot, Brisa, and Gil Sans.

Contents

Ring the bells that still can ring.
Forget your perfect offering.
There is a crack in everything.
That's how the light gets in.
—*From* Anthem *by*
Leonard Cohen

Prologue

A s YOU MAY HAVE GUESSED, the word *corner* is used in this book to represent our inner emotional experiences. Further, free verse that is focused on *habits* and *relationships*—both good and bad—is used to open these corners for our scrutiny and deeper reflection.

If you are holding this book, imagine your life as a series of corners...

And if you can imagine this, you know that some of your corners have been vibrant with happiness and triumphs while others have been darkened by dread and disappointment.

You may also be reminded of how you lingered too long in corners where you were hurt or contained. You may have fled others before you were fully loved or released into yourself.

Your corners, like mine, have involved the inevitable intersection of people and events. And our reactions to these people and events have ignited habits and relationships that served us well—or maybe not.

Section I, Habits, provides glimpses of real people who could not give up the force of their habits. Some had habits that, upon reading of them here, may inspire hopeful commitments to ourselves and others (Escaping the Corner, Homage to Mark, and Still Got Some Juice Left). Others' habits alert us to the inherent dangers of certain corners (Decision Time, Wild Horses, and Zoom Out).

In Section II, Relationships, many of these corners illuminate the sustaining power of loving and committed relationships (Vanishing, Mentor Missing, Unsaid, and Sudden Vase of Roses). Others convey the loss, torment, and grief of relationships gone awry (Lost Tango, Bell, and Final Ending).

Both of these sections are enriched by the magnificent illustrations of my colleague, Richard McKnight— illustrations that take us deeper into the corners we are exploring here.

In the concluding section, Commentaries, I make explicit the core messages embedded in the free verse. Some readers may prefer to start with a Commentary and then read the coordinated piece of poetry or prose. Others may prefer the reverse. It makes no difference. The point is this: that the reader is reminded of familiar corners and through those recollections emerge cues for sound life decisions now.

Finally, while the identities of the people who prompted

the exploration of these corners are protected, their habits and relationships are more universal than not. They are known to us. We have been in our own versions of these corners. We have blossomed in some, and have been lost in others. Escaping the Corner offers the possibility that if we choose to be mindful of these corners, we will recognize when it's time to linger in one — or, when it's really time to escape another.

Karol M. Wasylyshyn, PsyD
Philadelphia, PA
Fall, 2012

I. Habits

Today I Chased Some Words

Today I chased some words like every writer
chasing words into the night—drunk or sober
thinking the right words could be captured,
lined up, and made to surrender into lines
satisfying enough to continue.
I chased them around the curves
of my most taunting memories
and through the pages of Neruda, Rilke,
Yeats and Dickinson.

I lit a lavender candle in shameless adoration
and I relented to their power…falling into bed
pleading that they stop tormenting me with half
promises.

I cursed and crumpled them into a mess at my feet.
I read and re-read them until I couldn't see them clearly,
I threatened to expose them to all my limitations,
and finally, I even promised to lift them to the stars—
whenever my Muse arrived again.

Escaping The Corner

When did you see that red leaf
just wet from a quiet rain
a day or two away from its last season?
Or that silver green branch of fir
near caressing a mustard-colored wall?
Or the red lampshade…pristine and seductive
madly exhaling its light upward and
away from your lens that immortalized her?

You are red and green and mustard now
saturated by every shade and light,
infiltrated by the smells of the forest,
liberated over ocean and sand,
inebriated by the music of the barrio.
You are simultaneously fixated on the color of air
and caressing your wife's hands wet in the shapes
of her creations—even as you escape,
escape from the corner to discover yours.

The Tilt

The UFO glided to a soundless landing on the East River. It was a starless night after the ball had dropped in Times Square announcing the year 2012. Most revelers were still sleeping half loopy on champagne and other spirits—so no one noticed the arrivals who transformed themselves into a golden swarm of fireflies that night, and then a pink cumulous cloud blinking at dawn.

The evening fireflies and blinking cloud stayed for several days hovering over the city—observing and recording images of Manhattan's midtown occupants whom they came to call "the tilters." The visitors were bemused by many things. They noted how people crossed streets and walked together their heads bent forward at a perpetual 45 degree angle as they spoke into flat objects that made frequent pinging and ringing noises. They saw how this pinging and ringing commanded an immediate attention—a slight jerk of the upper body and then the tilted head.

They noticed a pattern whereby people used the flat object to speak with others who sat in places very close by. And

they witnessed most everyone spending hours in front of a screen with a keyboard below. From here they tapped messages to others sitting right behind them, studied words and images, and watched videos that made them laugh and even cry. Many bought books and music through the screen and sent electronic birthday greetings, too.

Apart from the tilters, they saw people walking everywhere lips moving talking to an invisible someone seemingly through a blue device in their ears. And still others were singing and snapping their fingers to silent rhythms the visitors could not hear. With great concern, they noted how people transported themselves through the city. Zipping behind and around each other their heads often in that forward tilt—their fingers simultaneously tapping on those same flat objects which meant their hands were never fully on the steering mechanisms of the vehicles they drove.

When the space travelers returned home, they beamed the collected Earth images to others in their solar system—all members of the Inter-Galactic Communication Council (IGCC). A huge debate ensued: Was the pervasive tilt a necessary aspect of Earthlings' communication? An irrepressible habit? Did it bring people closer together—or leave them apart?

Protect Me from What I Want

For all the talented people anywhere

all the talented people everywhere

who find what they want to be doing,

what they might even be meant to be doing —

there are a million hapless others,

zombies in glass towers

towers they couldn't resist,

zombies in mirrors in towers

or in taverns below towers,

often late in the tavern then

later…sleep walking on shifting, fallow ground.

Drenched

Drenched in after shave and pain,
more muddled than dumb or insane,
he ignores the lizard tail dangling,
from the briefcase on his hulk hanging,
as he plods toward the perch of his making,
a folly of ego forsaking,
any truth that wouldn't be speeding,
the story he'd always been feeding.

He doesn't hear his aimless mumbling,
or see at the mirror's edge crumbling,
the shattered shards of a life haunted,
more cobbled and riddled and gauntlet;
endless charade always right not aborted
flaccid story, nothing persuasive reported—
mighty protagonist and self-proclaimed winner
…but soon, very soon lizards' dinner.

Roar from the Canyon

There was no thirst in the canyon
        more persistent than yours—
you
        draining the stream
        and scanning the cliffs for take-off,
you
        stronger and longer
        in the taste of each essential milestone,
you
        traversing your way to the top of the canyon-
        coveted aerie there.
And surely,
        there was no louder roar
        reverberating through the canyon than
yours…
    after your rage lit the conflagration
        that brought you down.

Small Doses

Only the leather chairs in the airless, paneled room
could chronicle the decades with true accuracy;
self-possessed and comfortable as they were,
none saw the value in such truth-telling.

*Silent witnesses. We have never been summoned. Truth is for them
to discover. They will get to it—eventually. And if not, we will
have another group to seat.*

However, once—once when the room trembled
from a roar of pounding accusations, remonstrations,
when every chair's leather nearly split from the heat
of its occupants' outrage,
when some of them were sent careening on their sides,
and even the blinds shook in an undulation of disbelief,
the chairs' Chair demanded they speak.

In one trembling but persistent chorus of wooden voices
they whispered:

They can only take this leader in very small doses.

Float

One day he took a float unannounced

...loose in his mental caftan free

from the meetings, the meetings

choking his business with words.

Uncharted ride through the outposts

before the bugles could be sounded

or the lieutenants assembled for dinner.

Float, free float, free fall, free to see.

Listening with his eyes closed,

seeing with his nose flared open

tasting truth—fresh fruits from the field—

truth enough to set the course anew.

Decision Time

There is no more time.
You are out of time and
you must stop even the most
compelling excursions,
tempting diversions,
or local insurgencies
away from the core.

You are out of time
and the decisions,
the directions
for action, necessary action
must be orchestrated with
clarity and fierce will
over the oceans
where the waters have become
increasingly infested —
and you will soon be lunch,
and dinner.

Reading Bulls

He heard it on the news one night—

To fight a bull, you need to read a bull,

something about a bull-fighting school in America

where cape and eye were taught to meet the bull

where he had to be met lest too much form—

or even substance—sabotage a winning fight,

or risk savage gorings that rendered fighters

far more gutless, faithless, or art-less than they

already were.

They needed to have it all.

Burning Down the House

Only an owl outside
heard the collective wheezing
of the empty seats
in the darkened auditorium
where that morning's news
had sucked the place airless,
and sent employees packing
to vacate by the weekend.

The owl knew that too many
managers had mistaken
the quiet of those departing
as understanding,
and the busyness of those remaining
as commitment.

The owl knew, too that managers
had missed the chance
to reflect on their own failures,
to burn down the past and
to reconstruct a new house —
while there was still enough
time for people to enter it,
and feel empowered again.

Diving for Pearls

They were made to feel as precious as pearls—

Mikimoto's newly strung on a silken red cord

warm and glowing welcomed

into his legendary jewel box; great fanfare

and pageantry, the enormity of their beauty—

the Emeperor's treasures—golden cape of promise,

at least for a time, until he ripped the cord apart,

an inexplicable ripping, tears of pearls rolling down

and over the terrazzo floor—wet and luminous pearls

rushing to other boxes before his boots could crush them.

Man in the Mirror

He described it as one of the most stunning, most shocking, most traumatic moments of his adult life— washing his hands there in the men's lavatory at Manhattan's Rainbow Room. Stepping away from the

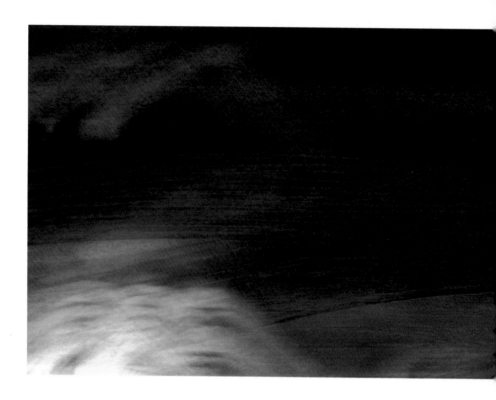

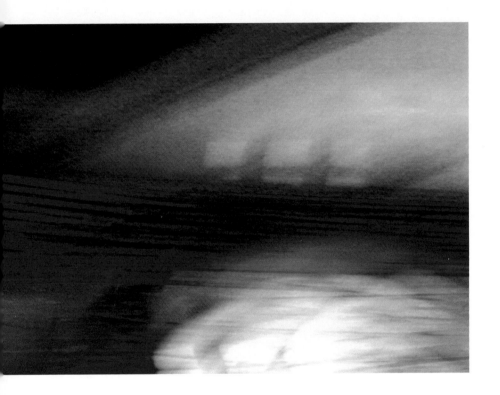

closeness of the person swaying a tad tipsy at the sink next
to his, annoyed at the intrusion of this man with the small
drip of red wine on his beige summer jacket—he focused
on the tired sagging face of the aging gentleman. Upon
realizing it was his, he bent over the wash basin weeping.

No Might This Night

Folly stopped pouring light into the cavern,
cavern of the monster, mad-minded monster
frozen heart, black-hearted crowded with demons
demons commanding the cavern with
needless distractions, heedless contractions
dark in the nights of his days parched and dry...
stark in the days of his nights drenched in suspicion.

Monster recharges...onto a new folly then—
Ah, luscious taste of the chase of new folly
new folly he immerses in fresh roses and wine
reckless, careless in the cavern cavorting
to his music...tango of words and false whispers
his body begs a dance, creeping shadow around her.

Monster dances enveloping new folly breathless
and molting...molting, she is alive and new:

Made
to
feel
flawless.

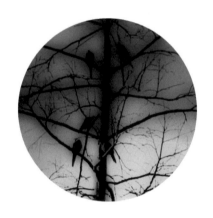

Folly is flawless—even into the moment
she is flung out, flung out in the midst of
their tango, mid-sentence above the dunes,
stars shrieking as he turns, dark spurn again.

Folly flung out, no candle to burn in the cavern
sealed over as steely eyes scan for his next chase
                        but monster tail flat…
                        monster is way out of might,
                                out of might,
                                out of sight…
                        out of time this night.

Zoom Out

When health cries Help! but goes unheeded,
it has no choice but to rip through the body
with a signal of such stunning magnitude
that the body's person is forced to a
full stop.

Quiet under the hospital sheet waiting
for results, treatment plan, prognosis,
the hated drag through recovery
as ego and mind battle, maybe reaching
compliance—or maybe not.

For some…well, slowing down to go fast
just isn't an option—not then, or ever.

Big Fish

Near the end of his sail, he swam into a cove

on a night when the moon bathed him in reflection.

He saw the dark in the dark as if it were light,

he heard the drum of his familiar evasions,

and the pulse of an anxious heart tightening

in his chest like wet sand. He had no answers,

he could not ease the force of the storm upon him

or evade its eye; unable to distract himself or

to swim any farther, he relented to his most

uneasy consideration: *What now?*

Running On Empty

He jogs at all hours,

beneath every tower,

half zombie, half sphinx

eyes hollowed out with no links

to his past—for he's set a new table,

lamentable cloth despite its fine label—

ever serving himself as main portion,

yesterday's lie…tomorrow's distortion.

Forest Moon

Step into the moonlight,

step into the moonlight,

stand close in the forest still.

Stand close in the forest still

until the certainty of what can be,

pierces and envelops you…

standing stiller

Still.

Tranquility Drive

Tranquility Drive—place or state of being?
Am I moving toward it? Am I on it? Near it? In it?
How does my life tally—the sum of its experiences
and loves worthy of more than mere remembrance?

A poet wrote,

Most things that are important, have you noticed,
lack a certain neatness.

But I am not untidy inside me or with the importance
of what surrounds me now;
it is a tranquil road I follow...
habits stacked neatly outside the closet for all to see.

The Night is Coming

He awakened to the cacophony of sea gulls,
gliding and landing on the beach,
then banking back over the water for breakfast.
So free and exuberant in their motion…
he swallowed them as moreNeruda moments;
he wanted to do to night what the sea gulls do to dawn.

Night has lost all its romance and subtlety for him now,
it has stopped easing in—
a thousand soft and indigo rose petals.

Night has become definitive, and oblivious—
not giving an owl's hoot
about anything he's done, or might continue
to discover for the world.

The Kingdom of Pace

The Kingdom of Pace was ruled by a King of distinctive and magnificent powers. The cascading force of his powers was so strong and relentless that none of his subjects could replicate them but they nevertheless persisted in trying to at least approximate his legendary capabilities. After all, the King rewarded them mightily to do so—they received significantly more gold and tools of their trade than did the subjects in any nearby kingdom. Further, on the extraordinary occasions when they met the King's expectations…a comforting glow of calm emanated from his chamber—and there was peace in the Kingdom for a time.

But the urgency for pace over-ruled peace in the kingdom. Not even the King's most talented subjects—his gifted Knights in Armor—escaped his chronic dissatisfaction regarding their speed and ability to meet his needs especially when he travelled to distant parts of the world. Even their best efforts to free the King of tasks that needlessly eroded his time were met with his derision or blocked by the King's insatiable need to control every facet of the kingdom. Often he railed about the knights' lack of planning or inability to identify the right problems to solve. His angry words would rain over them as sleet—but not even the most courageous among them could state the truth, "But King, you are so often the problem to solve."

The King became exceedingly more difficult to please and remote as he conquered other territories. While

questions about future plans for the kingdom persisted,
the King was disinclined to address his court enmasse. No
one understood why he refused this royal obligation. Some
Knights thought this was due to his innate shyness or his

naïveté about the power and importance of "live" ruler-to-
subject communication.

Others thought the King's quest for perfection—
his need to have the exact right words to describe his
expansion and vision for the kingdom—was at the core of
his not speaking publicly about it. And still others thought

it was his paranoid need to guard against anyone having full knowledge of his ideas. Whatever it was, the King's comfort with ambiguity—especially as it related to his plans for the kingdom—was infinitely greater than that of anyone else. Even his Chief Bursar was not privy to his plans, and there was no senior Council to advise or guide the King about them.

Eventually, even the King could not maintain the pace and quest for perfection that he believed were at the core of the kingdom's success. However, by that time the kingdom had achieved such legendary status it could thrive for awhile without his daily oversight. And while the King now seemed to have the personal time he always said he craved, he remained on his throne. He remained there and more aggressively extolled the accomplishments of his kingdom to envious others who travelled from afar to learn of them. And all the while, he continued to chide his loyal—and still infantilized—subjects for their failed efforts and lack of pace.

Once a chronicler was sent from abroad to meet with the King for an in-depth discussion of the kingdom's unparalleled success. He spent days with the King—days in rapt attention to how the kingdom had grown—and especially to how it had been ruled. The Chronicler's extensive essay appeared under the headline, The Incomparable Land of Eggshells. While the writer praised the King's brilliance and marveled at the stunning growth of the kingdom, he also challenged the King's harsh ways of ruling, and his adamant assessment that not one of his Knights could ever rule the kingdom as fully well as he.

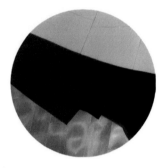

II. Relationships

A Team to Remember

Nine unlikely explorers boarded the boat with their bold and trusted Captain on their way to a new land. Without map, reliable compass, knowledge of the seas or local customs, they plotted and held a steady course — re-plotting rarely but always in synchrony with the moon lest they not leverage fast tides of good fortune. They grew to love the moon and the Captain, too for he could see beyond their self-imposed limitations and release their starlight, the starlight that produced their most skillful and passionate navigation.

Even when the seas turned brutal and their hands bled from the twisting ropes, all the days of twisting ropes that would have defeated most explorers, the Captain could still exhort their relentless efforts. At night, he would bandage each wounded hand personally, reminding the explorers about the bountiful land before them, how they would get there, and the joy they would feel when they arrived. Often they would celebrate, celebrate both progress and pain — celebrate late into the night with nourishing food and spirits, plentiful spirits and laughter heartier than the sea

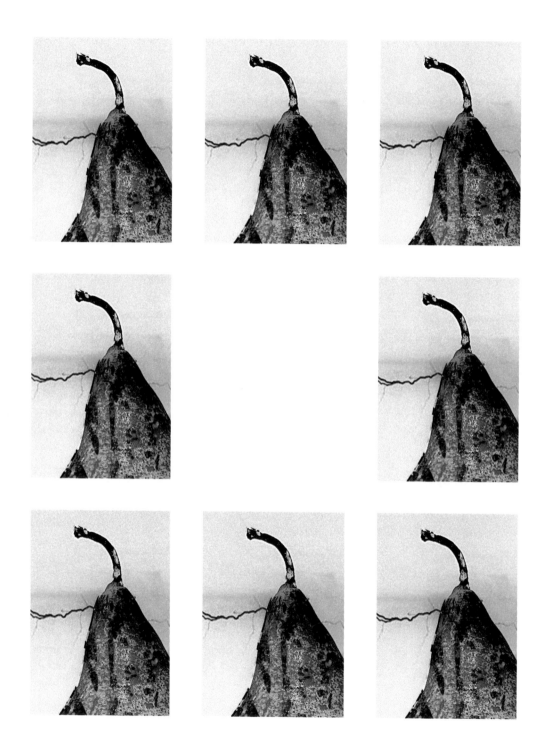

had heard from any band of explorers before them.

When these explorers reached the new land they sought, they claimed their distinctive place in it. They made reliable maps and charts for the future. They passed on their accumulated wisdom about the local customs, and they formed lasting friendships with the natives. But what they came seeking and found would always pale in comparison to what they had become in themselves—and together.

Vanishing

My most precious friend is vanishing,
and I howl against this here at his favorite
table in The Gramercy Tavern
table chosen for comfort and vista years ago,
but essential now lest I not hear him—
his 83-year old vocal chords
straining and I leaning over the table
my hair grazing his salad.

We are drinking champagne and Brunello
from a shot glass for him,
as he cannot tip his head back far enough for stemware.
Our conversation spills over the table,
words and tastes intermingling unlike before
when words trumped all flavors.
We are adrift in our memories,
this is the glow that binds us now.

My most precious friend is vanishing.
He cannot stand straight or sit easily,
his torso is sinking toward spine,
his quick mind is dimming at a hurried pace.

My most precious friend has been vanishing, the
physical and mental insults have been accumulating;
And I, well, I have begun to envision myself

sitting on a bench
in a silent stone courtyard,
hearing his words without him.

Still Got Some Juice Left

I'm struck by the sight of him…
red apron and slicked hair same color as his white shirt
neatly tucked but pulling across his chest
as he tries to get his aching knees to cooperate
bending slooooowly, to reach a bottom shelf there
at the Office Depot.
I hear him speaking a proper English,
patient and well-modulated even cheerful
alongside his sullen manager who's directing him,
manager with wayward hair dripping down
his back as a tail,
and a snake tattoo slithering up his arm to the jaw line.

Just as I start sinking into my melancholy version
of this senior's life, I see him laughing
and slapping his friend, Ralphie, on the shoulder;
they're talking about the Phillies and how
it's better to be out than in the house anymore—
especially since the wife…well, you know;
and they keep man-laughing and head-shaking
and holding just the right physical distance as they part
with him tapping Ralphie's arm, winking, and saying,
"I still got some juice left."

Mentor Missing

Walking home late from the office,
shoes soaked by a sudden rain,
she felt the cavernous space
of his absence.

Through the wet and the wind,
over the day and under the night
outside the inside of him
in that Square…where they'd sat,
the memorial flame now
cast a certain light,
and she could see the skin
of his glistened head
pulled across a brain
she craved to dissect.

Mentor, priest, seer,
and eternal friend —
dark, and luminous;
she longed for his return
to her confessional.

A Winter's Burning

Two friends have returned to their haunts

huddled in reunion but in a

distinctly different conversation now low

at the table where they are semi-drunk on

all the sonnets of their past—

and even more on what they will write

egos suspended, working together coherently

as one…lids of their mighty muse boxes

flung fully open to receive the burning flakes

of this winter's snow and promise.

Lost Tango

...anonymous sweat, small European hotel,
unhurried, not bartered or sullied or spoken,
hypnotic surrender ripped out of him,
silent tango melting over the sheet, sweet
tango half-crazed and titanic seduced then ...
until he'd had his fill of it.

Heart shrouded, iced over still years later
another dancing—sudden, unwanted
wanton envelopment...eruptive distraction,
fiercer steps, shoes gleaming on fireflies' light.
Free. Tedium made tolerable.
History revisited, renewed, reconstructed.
Better.

Disparate threads woven more tightly, new
partner holding his darkness, his eyes,
his mood, his brain, his beautiful ass ...
daring the sun to peel them,
peel them away from themselves
into each other without reason or parachute,
falling, falling from the moon, startled falling,
caressed falling, peeling, and falling still...even after.

Let the dinner burn...they're on the floor
one more frenzy, one more talk about

Bach and Oliver, Basho and Krall,
ardor filling this Darling destined to leave…
last dance before midnight,
last touch, last release, last moon,
last moon dance, the last of lasts…
before lasting into her own home.

Time into time later, heart frozen still,
ever stiller than his waning nights, he drifts…
deep in a tub at the foot of a mountain
snow falling, clouds cascading,
sake numbing all defenses, and
he sees an image lift through the thickening steam—
long body, strong hands moving toward his heart
green eyes caressing and he, stripped bare of
all suspicion and mime, knows that what he had
seduced and abandoned then…had been his truest tango.

Clearing Air...Like Roses

sweet

vibrant

no thorn

Unsaid

The small but majestic church
was caressed by stately pines
where it lived off a winding road
but where few came to sing,
or to inhale the smell of their faith shaken from the priest's
vessel and chain—
a swinging of intoxication and incantation…
rising above the pews bathed in vivid light
from window panes kaleidic color
depicting stories of God and his saints and angels.

This winter morning the little church yawns
in a death song; its doors open…
dark block of chocolate this building
in a crinoline of snow,
perfect setting for all its patient
and elaborate wood carvings to be seen and admired—
Not a nail in the place someone says—
except in the coffin, but that's another story.

Anything left unsaid sprang from the son's tenor voice
in full andmagnificent crescendo intermingling with
the smoke and the light and the carvings without nails—or
hands to touch them.

Invention

Do you remember how after—after the electricity,

the great conflagration that nearly burned you down—how

you couldn't even recall the spark?

You remembered only that something wild and

ill-formed arrived—unwieldy mass of clay that yielded

to your kneading and throwing and molding on the wheel,

you imagining a vessel, a vessel beyond its own words or

thoughts, briefly perfect vessel tempting for a time in its

persistence, beckoning shades of blue and promise,

well-fated vessel for drinking—tipping with you all numb

and crazy…sliding into your next night.

Brief night. Yes.

Yes, sometimes we invent what we need.

Flaming Lips

The stream of her words had a strange beat,
starting slowly…halting then steady, steady
first as a starling's wings…quiet whispering
incoherent, lost but seeking absolution…or,
at least a linen envelop to hold her obsession.

Then as the flapping of a gull, loud nude flapping,
words whipping sand in the face of reason…open
screeching, reaping a samba shock and swiftness
her torments tumbling out uncensored—and proud;
she cannot cease the telling of her lurid injuries.

And finally, as the full spreading of a raptor's wings,
raptor diving and spewing words, words on fire
howling beat from the jungle of her soul pounding
from the temple where she strides up to Mother and
taunts with a kiss, *Now it is my turn to burn you down.*

An Homage to Mark

I am only as certain as all the uncertainties
that have been vetted with you, me naked
in front of the mirror you hold with tender
allegiance…and honesty.

I am only as right as all the wrong-headedness
that you have patiently considered and rejected
deftly maneuvering me back to where I started
before I exposed my fleeting bits of stupidity.

I am only as clear as my unintended vagueness
producing that odd knitting of your eyebrows
and then our rational syncopation helping me
produce more coherent communication.

I am only as visionary as all my tactical updates
that have lost your attention as you ask, What's next?
and I'm forced to abandon my trusted checklists
and finally put a courageous idea on the table.

I am only as courageous as my stubborn fears
that you readily hoist and pierce with the history
of my risks well-taken and won despite the
faithless odds I gave myself.

I am only as empowering as the disempowering pucks
you bring and place at my feet as a loyal pet reminding
its master that others want to get on the playground, too
and that that is the best game for all of us.

I am only as motivating as my most de-motivating actions
actions you catch with your vigilant butterfly net
reminding me of how weird and self-important I can be
even as I promise others' growth and engagement.

I am only as reflective as the cacophony in my head
the multi-tasking you monitor and ease with direction
away from the BlackBerry head tilt and audible pings
that have taken command of my consciousness.

I am only as empathic as all my unintended gaffes
that you see in the hurried emails fired off at night
to the sleeping who have dismissed my latest messages
about maintaining focus and accountability.

I am only as contented as my most discontented manager
buried in work that you point out she shouldn't be doing
because I have skipped her last performance review
trusting her new raise is sufficient reward of her talents.

I am only as grateful as my most ungrateful moments
too frequent you remind me with serious caution
your wisdom pouring over me, as into a vessel waiting

to be filled, but never savoring enough of what has been.

I am only as balanced as the truth of my unbalanced life—
this you chase with great vengeance and fear knowing
that my partner, other loved ones—and my health, too
may not wait for me to complete this working.

Ode to JTB

Sweet jive jam

jumpin' Jack Johnny

jumpin' on her bed

delirious!

Thank You, Anais Nin

Tonight she drinks champagne,
forcing reason to bleed out
leeching her free
free to sip times ago,
when blooming night orchids
faded warm into mornings.

Tonight she can recover
another scent of it—there
where a cold Maine whisper
hovered over the bed sheeting
entreating their timid discovery
of how to entwine with another.

Tonight she drinks champagne,
emotions flooding in
the din…of her more free
free, in strips of time ago
re-visiting…
every touch—an ember's glow.

P'Town, 2007

Adrift in Provincetown, more
Beautiful aging men than I can
Count—though
Decidedly apart from my
Erotic preferences or
Fantasies
Grooved far from this
Hand-holding capital of America
Indescribably abandoned unto itself with
Just-in-time juices sufficient to
Keep even the
Loneliest cowboy quenched at
Midnight when
Names—names never matter and
One man's repetition is another's
Possibility
Quick
Rhapsodic fade to
Sleep
Tongue finally still after its
Undulations
Very
Wet this
Xerox moment
Yearning for its own
Zoo-bi-lee.

Janitor's Son

He tried to honor the sweep of his father's broom,
exhorting him to believe that he was way more
than the sum of his circumstances…

or got distracted, or took a wrong turn and got lost
when it was supposed to see his father's possibility.
Janitor's son pleaded—needed for father
to lift from the basement for himself, and for son
who craved one gaze of encouragement.

But father would not be convinced of himself,
or trust, or take pride in the pursuits of his son—
son's steady course away from the table,
kitchen table where primal issues trumped
father and son love.
Father morose and quiet at the table—
an emotional tide of neglect, son near drowning
but swimming, swimming away from the table.

I am my father's son; but I am not lame inside me.
Nor is he gone outside me. We are one with this broom.
It has swept us together into our steady corner;
I have lit incense and an eternal flame there.

Son continues a fervent sweeping and steeping of time,
time reassembled and corrected—time for safe-keeping,
new time of clearing and piling abundance on the table—
table where his own sons are ripened for reaping.

A Sudden Vase of Roses

If more men understood that it is

the suddenness of the roses,

hidden behind a lamp

in the bedroom when

women least expect it—

that can turn a question

into the certainty of a future

at least for a time,

a time of roses now,

and fond reverie later—

If more men understood this

then, well wouldn't it all be

so much easier?

Nearest

Somewhere over the Pacific,

he shifted restlessly in his seat

wondering how badly

his work would scar them:

When are we nearest, Sweet Heart?

Evenings ago skin on skin?

Or now, in this distance

tethered by words?

Bell

Who is the bell?

Who is the clapper?

When it's gone silent …

Where is the music?

Tongues Misbehave

Absent of grace,
or light,
or music,
most of the angry words
tumble into a darkened canyon
piling onto each other
in a dirge.

They cannot sing
or lift a glass of wine in
celebration—
they cannot see another way,
or dine on
the taste of elation.

They are dry
lonely and pointless,
but still hurled
by certain tongues...dauntless.

Held Hostage

In a British Airways First Class lounge, she observed an animated business executive on his mobile saying something that went like this: *It was like the vibrancy of a great painting, a tango, and a Beethoven Symphony all rolled into one!*

Unable to suppress her curiosity, when she met him at the coffee station she inquired about what he meant. He smiled broadly answering, *That's the atmosphere you create in your leadership team when you finally get rid of the hostage taker— that arrogant, self-centered little blocker. I could add a few expletives, but you get the drift.*

And she did.

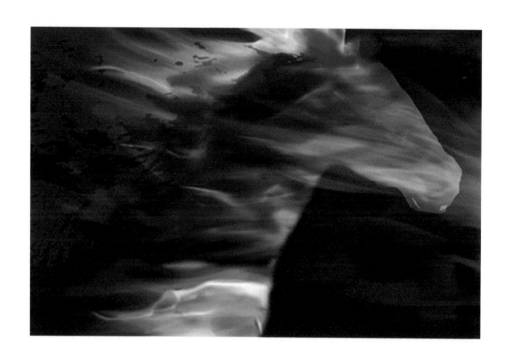

Wild Horses

Howdy partner—hey you, there beside

the ambitious Other, the soaring Other

half present at the family table

where every ping! produces a Tourette's moment—

even on vibrate—the family sees its power trumping

all their efforts at having a real conversation.

You go out riding in a pack or alone, don't you?

Fierce riding in the afternoons

through promenades thick

in silk and lavender…

and wine from the caverns where some riders drift and

lift—into the creation of the partners they crave.

Gone

...another friend gone;

brazen wind,

barren day,

scentless air,

and buried roses.

I am veering

between

wild stallion...

and nun.

30-Mile Veil

He had good equipment to fly in it,

around it, even high over it,

and low under the legs of it,

but never lastingly within it…

tangled tresses and truths,

tattered veils

twisting and binding him

in ghosts.

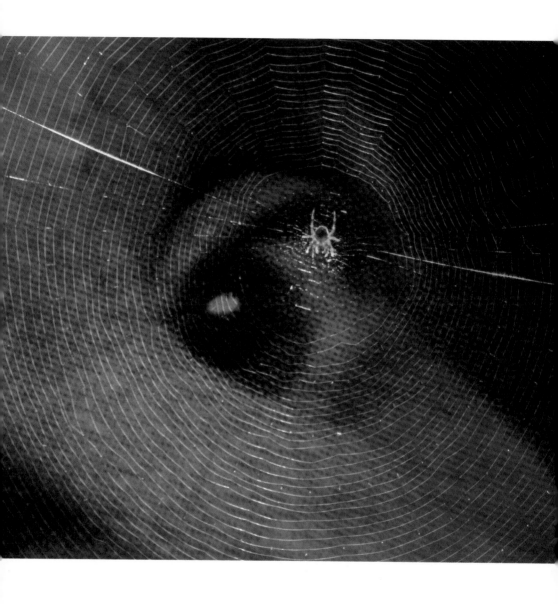

Final Ending

It is as a spider creeping out
from its web in the corner,
creeping over the blanket
and under the sheet steady
and strong in its mission —
watching their empty kisses,
their restless bodies now
aware that the darkness has become
too thick between them...
and something is keeping the distance
cold from the warmth that had
pervaded a perfect beginning.

They arise stung and wrung out —
sleepless from the stillness
of the nights so long in the silent
agony of a present gone dry,
and a future soaked in the flood
of this final ending.

Commentaries

I. HABITS

Today I Chased Some Words

Creative pursuits such as writing can press one into corners of particular dread—and triumph. From catalytic moment to a work's completion, finding the right words or waiting for the Muse to arrive challenges every writer. However, when it happens, when the words are finally found, and when they actually get woven into lasting moments of meaning for reflection, then the torturous process of getting there becomes a reward in and of itself.

Escaping the Corner

Among the most fortunate retiring business leaders are those who escape the corners of their corporate lives and pursue creative endeavors that may have been dormant for some time. In this poem, a retired Human Resources executive, generalizes his eye for talent and organization functionality to photography. Within a short time, he becomes a gifted photographer.

The Tilt

From the perspective of human communication, research on the impact of information technology and its attendant habits presents mixed results. Some studies suggest people have been drawn closer through it while other data indicate that the rates of isolation, alienation and depression are higher now than at any time in our society.

15

17

18

23

Protect Me from What I Want

This poem was inspired by the artist and designer, Tobias Wong, who tattooed the words *Protect me from what I want* on his arm. While his partner maintained that Wong hung himself while sleep-walking, the details of this suicide were never fully clarified. Wong's words prompt many questions including: How many of us get the work we thought we wanted only to become mired in habits akin to a kind of living suicide?

24

Drenched

In his youth, this business manager had aspired to become a professional athlete. However, an early injury forced a Plan B. While he adjusts with a modicum of success, he is stuck in a delusion about his potential—a potential that is diminished each time he fumbles another presentation in front of senior management.

27

Roar from the Canyon

Having long aspired to become a CEO, this gifted executive was days away from achieving his goal. However, unable to control his volatility, he explodes in a Board meeting, and ultimately someone else is appointed CEO. The ill-fated executive leaves the company within weeks—never to achieve his aspiration.

29

Small Doses

Advancing on the strength of their innate brilliance and business acumen, many corporate executives are otherwise limited—especially in terms of emotional self control. While they can turn on a certain degree of charm—especially with important external stakeholders—they can also "lose it" in sudden, inexplicable outbursts inside their companies.

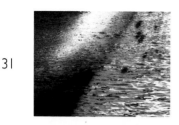

Float

31

His leadership team stuck in habits and a strategy that isn't working, this General Manager decides to visit the field with the intention of seeing things for himself and to use what he learns as the basis for setting a revised course of action.

Decision Time

32

Among the most frequent—and potentially fatal—habits of even senior executives is their failing to remain in strategic alignment with top management and therefore, not delivering on expected results. This is especially challenging in global companies where local conditions or priorities can compete with, resist, or otherwise distract one from making necessary and timely decisions.

Reading Bulls

35

Difficult to succeed in the current business climate without being well-attuned to the "bulls" in one's market—be they actual people or other problems to solve. While the behavioral "reading" aspect of doing business is less evolved for some, it has become as essential as other good leadership habits. Top leaders need to have it all.

Burning Down the House

36

It's a dark time for employees whenever a company initiates a reduction in force (RIF). Smart companies strive not to repeat the past, focus on the managerial "lessons learned," and take steps to help motivate the "survivors."

Diving for Pearls

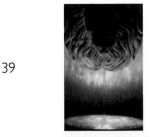

39

A brilliant entrepreneur had a pattern of hiring stellar consultants who helped him distinguish his firm and create a national entity. However, given the intensity of his sudden, mean and irrational temper flares, he was not able to retain the most talented among them.

Man in The Mirror

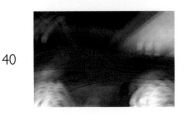

40

This CEO had long been the handsome and quintessential dashing man-about-town. Experiencing his aging as an intense narcissistic insult, he began to drink more heavily as he neared retirement. While others described him as an alcoholic, he rationalized the drinking as his way of "dealing with the inevitable."

No Might This Night

43

In this leader's secret personal life, his inner "demons" of mistrust, lust, and paranoia, render him incapable of sustaining a mature and committed relationship. A habitual thrill seeker, he lives in a corner where his ego is fed by a series of romantic conquests. He plays an enigmatic and repetitive game of seduction and rejection. In the end, however, this aging lothario would have to confront the fading of his seductive power and its depressing effects.

Zoom Out

47

Many business leaders refuse to make the necessary lifestyle adjustments warranted after physical incidents like heart attacks or bouts with other life-threatening diseases. Instead, they play a fatalistic game by defending against these warning signals with redoubled efforts at work.

Big Fish

49

Like many senior executives who have defined themselves primarily by what they do, this man is about to retire but without the benefit of having planned his life's next chapter. This has raised a level of concern and even fear that out-shadows any of the business issues with which he contended so capably.

Running on Empty

50

Now retired, this former corporate executive has no intention of greeting anyone—not even past colleagues whom he passes on his daily jogs through the city. And in his personal life, he continues as the self-absorbed host he'd always been.

Forest Moon

53

Plagued by self doubts and procrastination, this corporate lawyer began to envision the end stage of his career—and what he wanted to be able to say when he got there. That clarity helped him pull out of bad habits that eroded the likelihood of his achieving his aspirations.

Tranquility Drive

54

On the way into Cape May, New Jersey there is a small road named Tranquility Drive. For a retired insurance executive, who lives in the area, this name prompted his quick mental inventory of the life he's made with his partner, their habits, and the values they share. The line of poetry italicized here is from Mary Oliver's, The Bleeding Heart.

The Night is Coming

57

Night serves as a metaphor for death in these spare lines focused on the final days of an accomplished research scientist. Completely self-absorbed, dismissive, and irascible throughout his career, he is ill-equipped to deal with the feelings of loss and futility washing over him as he lay dying

The Kingdom of Pace

58

In this allegory, we are reminded that Founder CEOs often build extraordinarily successful businesses that continue to thrive when they remain in full command of them. However, their massive egos as manifested in behaviors that include intellectual arrogance, dominance, hyper criticism of others, and an excessive need to control can jeopardize the perpetuation of the enterprise. From a talent management perspective, these behaviors can prevent them from developing the next generation of talented managers and from planning an orderly succession.

II. RELATIONSHIPS

A Team to Remember

64

The memory of having been part of a great team—a group of dedicated colleagues that delivered something distinctive and commercially successful—can linger and produce instantaneous recall. Often, when people are asked about such an experience, they will point first and fondly to the exceptional skill of the team's leader who melded them into a passionate team that worked and played harder than any one of them imagined possible.

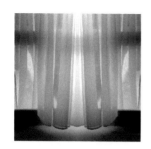

Vanishing

The inevitability of loss pervades this poem reminding us of the finite quality of life and the need to prepare ourselves for the relationship losses that will hurt the most. This woman can no longer deny the truth of her former boss's physical and mental deterioration. She moves toward accepting his decline but also toward a vision of how she will keep his voice alive inside her.

Still Got Some Juice Left

Retirement—one of life's toughest transitions—plays out in unexpected ways for most. Some never quite recover from losing the habit of work and they become lost, inert. Others find ways to just keep working— working at anything, it doesn't really matter what it is.

Mentor Missing

A business manager is reminded of—and longs for—the presence of a mentor whom she reveres. While she respects him for what he's taught her, she admires him more for the many roles he's played and the non-judgmental haven he's represented in her life.

A Winter's Burning

Two former colleagues are reunited and ignited by the possibility of collaborating together. They discover that what they can write together in this newly discovered corner is unlike anything either of them could have produced alone.

Lost Tango

This poem builds on the theme of anonymous carnality as plumbed in Bernardo Bertolucci's brilliant film, *Last Tango in Paris*. A lonesome business executive is suddenly seized—and briefly opened—by a romance of astounding power. While he must pursue it, he cannot sustain it or believe in its possibility. Near his life's end, alone in a rare mood of honest reflection, the repressed memory of this relationship is released—enveloping him in its truth and melancholic magnitude.

Clearing Air...Like Roses

In the aftermath of an argument or estrangement when the air between two people—either in a work-related or personal relationship—is finally and fully cleared, all things seem possible.

Unsaid

A CEO and only son is at his mother's funeral where both the ritual and the holy place in which it is held evoke his strong emotion— evident most through his voice in the portion of the mass he sings.

Invention

How do we understand our attraction to unlikely others? What's going on when the idealized "other" is far less real than the version of him/her that's been conjured in our heads? For many, the inexplicable other is not more than one's just-in-time creation of a place, a passageway, a necessary launching pad into the next life phase.

78

81

83

85

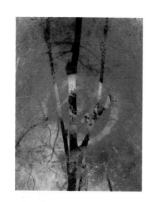

Flaming Lips

This scientist has achieved notable success despite the traumatic events of her childhood. Having endured her mentally ill mother's emotional and physical abuse—including a reported attempt to burn down the house in which she and her younger brother were left alone—she frequently, eagerly describes the horrific events of her early years. Mommy Dearest's heinous acts are worn as daughter's badge of survival and, fuel her matricidal fantasies.

An Homage to Mark

Behind most effective leaders there is a trusted go-to person or two, i.e. individuals who will tell-it-like-it-is, make sure the leader doesn't fall victim to his/her press clippings, and reinforce the leader's best habits by holding up a mirror with equal measures of truth, caution, admiration, and encouragement.

Ode to JTB

First loves have varying effects. For some, these experiences get stored in corners as relationship bench marks, intoxicating memories to savor, or clues for future relationships. For others, they fuel a chronic sense of unrequited love.

Thank You, Anais Nin

Drawn briefly into a reverie of past intimate experiences, this business woman faces the passage of time. She evades its diminishing effects with a good champagne and a particularly well-cherished memory.

P'Town, 2007

While in uber gay-friendly Provincetown at the tip of Massachusetts on Cape Cod, the author once saw a male corporate executive holding hands with another man. In response to his look of panic, she customized a familiar expression saying reassuringly, "What happens in Provincetown stays in Provincetown."

Janitor's Son

A tormented, dark side of the universal immigrant strive-for-success theme is revealed through the conflict of this father and son. The working class father cannot transcend his anger and self revulsion, nor can he take active interest in or savor the accomplishments of his only son. Ultimately, the son's self compassion helps him reframe the struggle with his father as a positive in his own development, as well as in the loving of his own sons.

A Sudden Vase of Roses

The element of surprise—the beauty and seduction of an unexpected gesture—is revealed here as the turning moment in the quest for a woman's attention and eventual affection.

Nearest

This newly married executive, already divorced once, hopes he'll not repeat history in his current marriage. He has forced himself to be more expressive, as well as to maintain frequent communication with his second wife especially when he travels on extensive business trips.

Bell

105

This small meditation on the sudden and oft misunderstood silences that creep into a relationship reminds us perhaps that remembering the music, staying focused on getting back to it, and discovering whether there's any music left at all are more productive pursuits than dwelling on who's the clapper or who's the bell when communication has gone cold.

Tongues Misbehave

107

When it comes to differing views in business, where is the nobler intention—in the fight , or in the quest for understanding?

Held Hostage

109

It only takes one powerful—but non-team oriented—member of a senior leadership team to sabotage its best efforts. When CEOs are asked what they might have done differently during their tenures, one of the most common replies is how they wished they had moved sooner on the removal of such people.

Wild Horses

111

Information technology has—simultaneous with its positive commercial effects—spawned habits of great negative consequence in the families of business leaders. Spouses and children can grow resentful of its intrusion into family time. Out of ennui, frustration, emptiness, loneliness, spiteful anger or elements of any of these in combination, some afternoon riders can get into the habit of hitching up to others.

113

Gone

In the wake of a number of friends' deaths, this accomplished woman is feeling bereft—and stuck in a conflict between just letting loose and living life more fully or reining in her impulses completely.

114

30-Mile Veil

As successful as this freelance pilot was in business, his life was littered with broken personal relationships including three divorces. Smart, handsome, and creative, he fared well in the early stages of a romance but he persisted in behaviors that shred them into tatters over time.

117

Final Ending

An executive couple drifting apart for years, faces the end of their relationship.

Artist's Statement
Richard McKnight

TYPICALLY, WHEN PRODUCING MY ART, I do not have an end in mind, rather striving for a result that is both beautiful and edgy, sweet and disturbing, mirroring how I see life itself. Most of my images are surreal, i.e., a blend of the actual and the imagined, the abstract and the literal, the sublime and the ridiculous.

When people see my work, my fervent hope is that they become caught up for a moment in a place that has no words, a place filled with wonder, awe, and harmony—even if what they're looking at is that picture with the spider on p. 117. I want to stop people in their tracks.

Many of these images are available as fine art prints at
RichardMcKnight.com.

Notes

Notes

We produce and market inspiring books for those who seek to embrace life enthusiastically, possess boundless vitality, and address challenges confidently. To inquire about bulk orders, visit us online at TrueNorthPress.com.

CPSIA information can be obtained
at www.ICGtesting.com
Printed in the USA
LVIW010423081212

310573LV00005B